KEEPING MINIBEASTS

W9-ABR-749

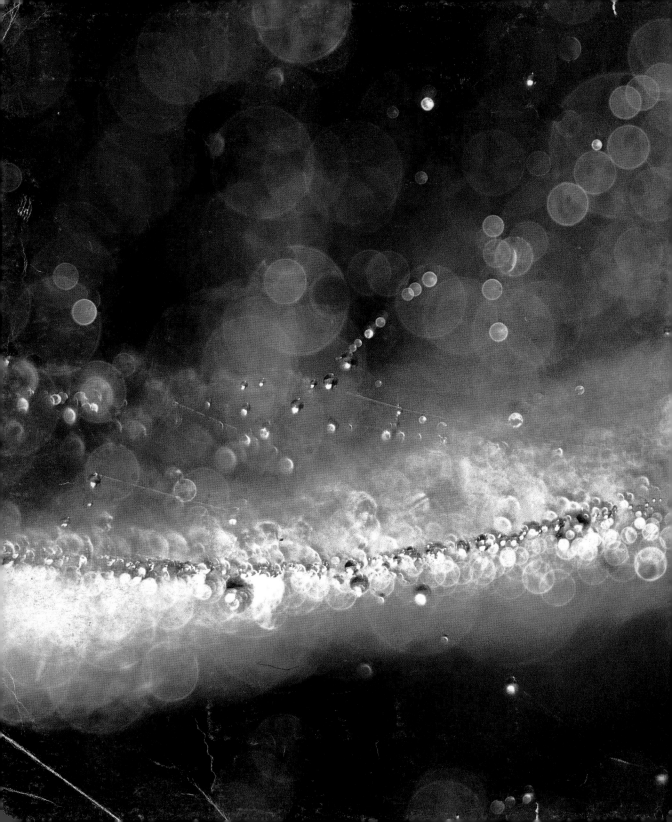

© 1988 Franklin Watts

First published in Great Britain in 1988 by
Franklin Watts
12a Golden Square
London W1

First published in the USA by
Franklin Watts Inc.
387 Park Avenue South
New York, NY. 10016

First Published in Australia by
Franklin Watts Australia
14 Mars Road, Lane Cove
New South Wales 2066

UK ISBN: 086313 694 X
US ISBN: 0-531-10642-X
Library of Congress Catalog
Card No: 88-50366

Design: Ben White

Printed in Italy by G. Canale & C. S.p.A. Turin

ISBN 0-531-15624-9 (pbk.)
First Paperback Edition 1991

Special thanks are due to Kathleen Hancock of
Tarantulas Etc. for all her help in the preparation
of this book.

KEEPING MINIBEASTS

SPIDERS

TEXT: CHRIS HENWOOD

PHOTOGRAPHS: BARRIE WATTS

CONTENTS

FRANKLIN WATTS

LONDON • NEW YORK • SYDNEY • TORONTO

Introducing spiders

People have many different feelings about spiders. Some people like them, but many are frightened by them. Before you decide to keep any spider, check that no one in your family has a fear of spiders.

Spiders are not insects. They belong to a group of animals known as arachnids. Spiders are measured by the length of their bodies and not the distance between their legs.

Habitats

Spiders are found in most parts of the world, except in the cold polar regions. Some live in houses, gardens and woods. Other spiders live in tropical forests, hot deserts and even under water.

Some spiders build webs or tunnels or traps. They live under rocks and logs, in buildings, hedges, caves and tall trees.

Dangerous spiders?

All spiders have poison glands but only a very few are dangerous to humans. Usually the poison, called venom, works only against small creatures which are food for the spider.

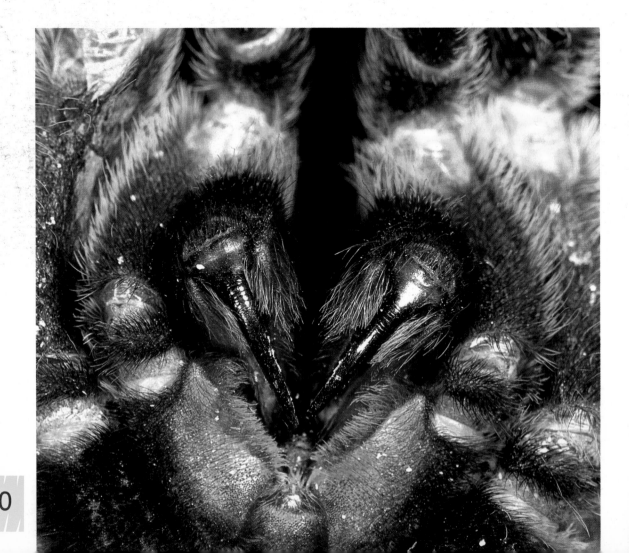

Even the bite of a Tarantula is no more dangerous than a wasp sting. But the Tarantula's fangs look very vicious. Many people are bitten by spiders but most people don't even know!

Handle with care

The best way to pick up a spider is to use a scoop of some type. An empty can or plastic cup is good.

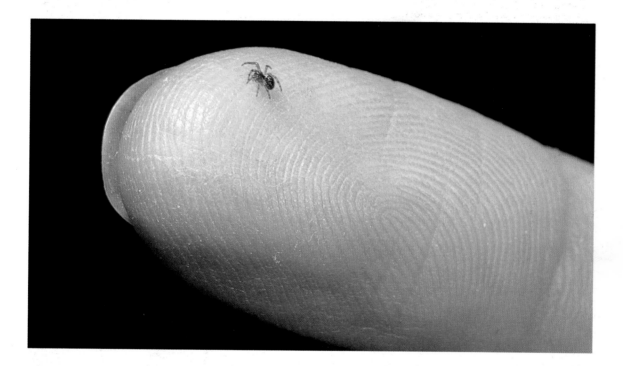

Some spiders, like Tarantulas, have bristles on their legs. These bristles break off very easily and can cause a bad rash. Small spiders should be handled very gently.

Collecting spiders

Small, common spiders can be collected easily by carefully knocking them into a jar or plastic container. They must be treated gently.

When capturing your spider be very careful
not to damage it. Don't let it bang against the
side of the container. Try to allow it to lower
itself by its own silk thread.

Housing

Most common spiders are quite happy to live in a small, plastic fish tank, with a plastic or cloth mesh top. Put some litter on the bottom of the tank. You could use gravel or sand.

Most larger spiders will enjoy a dark place under which to hide. This can be half a flower pot, a piece of bark or cardboard. From time to time spray the inside of the tank with water.

In the wild, spiders eat a wide variety of foods. Many of these foods are insects that can be harmful to humans.

Most spiders will eat mosquitoes, moths, houseflies, butterflies and caterpillars. Some large spiders such as Tarantulas will attack and eat small mammals and even small birds.

Diet in captivity

If kept in captivity, the spiders' diet should be as near natural as possible. They are interested only in food that moves, so you must give them live food.

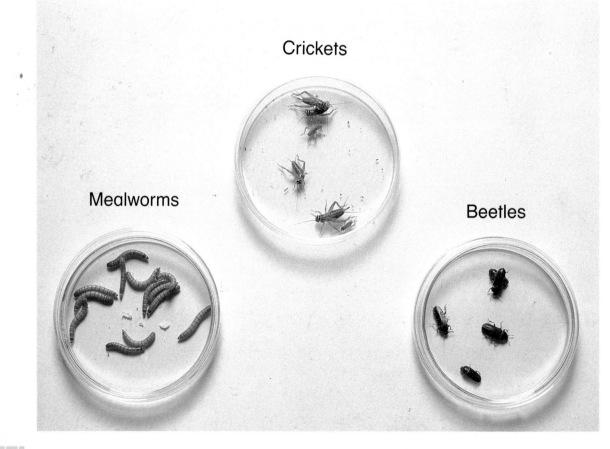

Crickets

Mealworms

Beetles

Flies, mealworms and small crickets can be
used to feed your pets. You can also capture
insects from the house or garden. Be careful
not to collect insects from places that have
been sprayed with chemicals which kill insects.

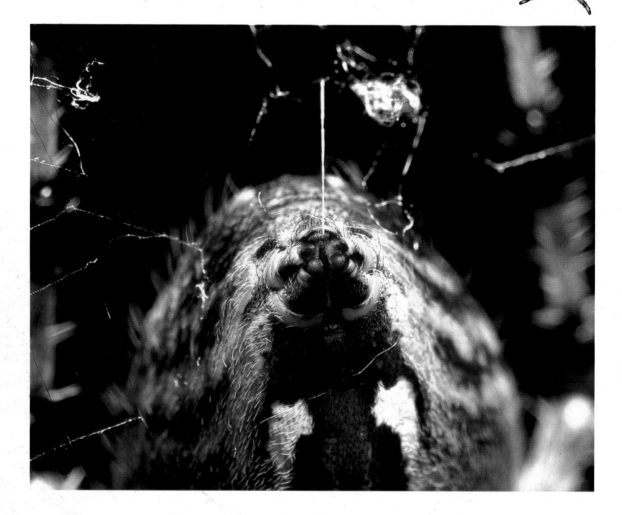

Although all spiders can spin and produce silk, not all spiders build webs in which to trap other animals.

Spiders are separated into a number of groups based on the type of silk traps they produce.

Sheet webs are often found in corners of buildings and trap non-flying insects.

More webs

Orb webs are the most familiar although no two orb webs are alike. Orb webs are often found strung between bushes like large fishing nets. They trap flying insects day or night.

This is a hammock web. The spider waits underneath for the insect to walk on top of the web then grabs it and paralyzes it.

Releasing your spiders

When you go away you really don't have to worry about finding someone to look after your pet spider for you. Providing it is a species that you obtained locally from the

wild, you can always release it back to where you first caught it. Of course, you should only do this when the weather is warm.

Unusual facts

There are over 30,000 recognised species of spider in the world today, with new species still being discovered each year.

At certain times of the year, there may be over two million spiders in every acre of land in some places.

Male spiders always have smaller bodies than female spiders. They are often very much smaller so that in some species the males become meals for the females.

Spiders are not insects and have eight legs with a body divided into two parts.

Some spiders that don't make webs catch their prey by chasing it, jumping on it or ambushing it.

Index

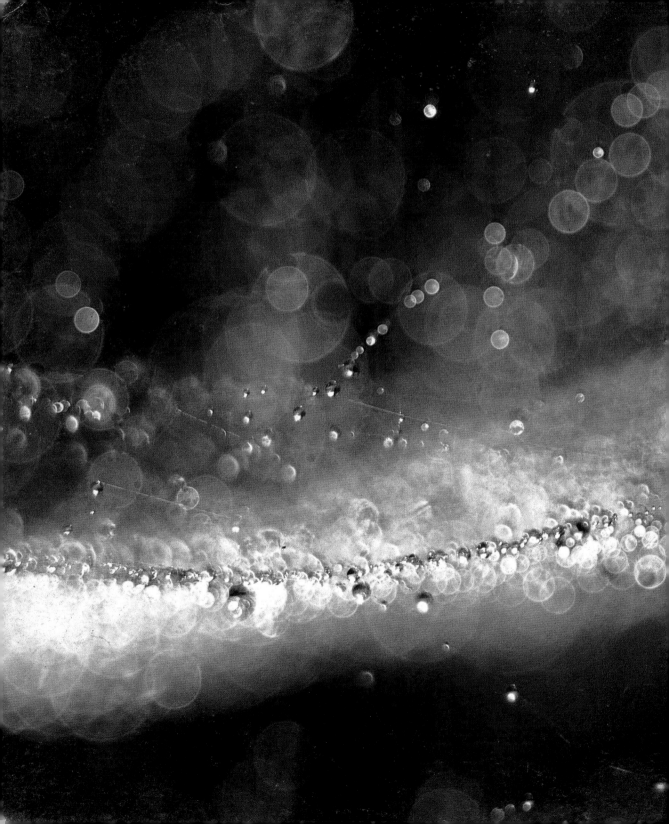

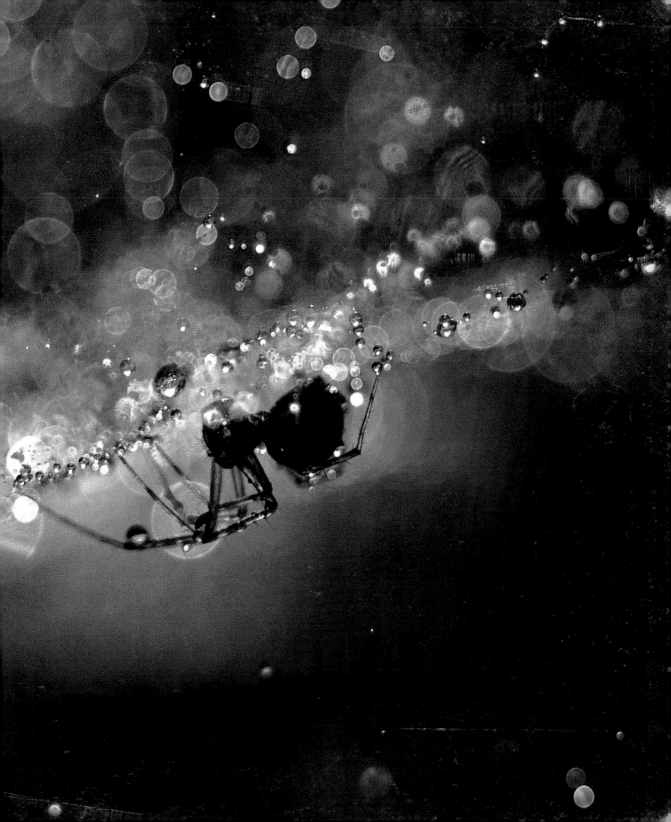